U
KNOW
U
CAN GO
THE
DISTANCE

A DISTINCTLY DIFFERENT BOOK
[PERSONAL DEVELOPMENT & MOTIVATION PUBLICATION]

U
KNOW
U CAN GO
THE
DISTANCE

by
AH-TT

Published By
DISTINCTLY DIFFERENT BOOKS AND PUBLICATIONS
29 Dairy Close, Willesden, London NW10 3RJ

The author, editor and publisher would like to thank the following for
permission to quote from copyright material: Edward de Bono

Illustrations in Colour
Illustrations © Tolu Shofule

Set in Tahoma
Printed and Bound in Great Britain by
AXIS EUROPE PLC
Unit 7 Higgs Industrial Estate
Herne Hill Road
London SE24 0AU

This book is dedicated to the memory of two very special men whose lives have inspired me greatly.

They went through life seeing every challenge as one more opportunity to unfold their passion to achieve:

Emmanuel

and

Isaac

ACKNOWLEDGEMENTS

I give all the glory to my Lord God for filling me with the inspiration and confidence to write this book.
I am a seed sower through motivational messages and I do not attempt to limit the power or reduce the significance and purpose of God in our lives.
I use my writing talents to attest to the goodness of my Lord.

Thanking;
My husband Dele and my 6 wonderful children for all their love, tireless patience and endless support...

'Without you all, I am incomplete'

I thank...
Errol Williams for making me see the value of transforming my message into a book

Aunty Imasuen Wallace, Muni King, Rick Lynch, Steve McCurly, Tunde Fagbenle, and Rebecca Thurgur for reading the initial drafts and providing editing advice, encouragement and invaluable feedback

Tolu Shofule for using his gift to translate the message in this book into illustrations and for giving his precious time, energy, support...

Brian Parish, Simon Gill, Les Streater and the team at AXIS EUROPE PLC [Printing Division], for you all it's more than printing, it's your passion

Mummy, My Sister Eki Gbinigie, Aunty Susan Onosode, Ngozi Egenti, Chinyere Egenti, Kamillah Huggins, Remi Oloko, Femi Elias, Kayode Ogunlesi, Andrew Owen-Grey, Ann Oboth, Michelle Jimenez, and Monica Banatova for confirming what I've always felt...

The need to write this message as I have done, making it

Clear and **Uncomplicated** just for **U**.

U KNOW U CAN GO THE DISTANCE

When I say that U know U can go the distance, your first response will probably be to smile to yourself wryly as U reflect on what U perceive to be that *mountain* of hurdles that U have got to overcome in your life, and U probably say to either yourself, or me ...

'What do U know about my life'?

or

'Who do U think U are to tell me I can go the distance?
U don't know what I've been through nor what I've got to get through in my life'

And in this U are absolutely right, but guess what? ... It doesn't matter what I do or do not know about **YOUR LIFE**, it's what I know about U that U need to realise about **YOURSELF** and this is the fact that U have:

• the potential

• the ability

and

• what it takes to achieve, succeed, get **where** U want or get **what** U want.

Ask me how I know?

Because ...

I BELIEVE IN U, NOW U NEED TO START BELIEVING IN YOURSELF!

Since we often spend the better part of our lives doubting ourselves, and what we **ARE** capable of achieving, we need to spend some time mending the way we have been thinking **HEALING OUR THOUGHTS** shifting from SELF-DOUBT to **SELF-BELIEF**.

AH-TT

In the words of ...

'U can analyse the past
but,
U have to design the future'.

'If U do not design the future,
someone or something else
will design it for U'.

... Edward de Bono

CONTENTS

THE BEGINNING

'the best place to start'

STAGE ONE   REFLECT

Taking Stock -
[quit dwelling and moping]

Without sounding too philosophical if U don't know where you're coming from how on earth can U plot your path to where you'd like to go?

HELLO! Reality Check Time!

That is what U will be doing as U read through this reflection stage.

U will reminisce about all the things U have done in your lifetime, as you've grown from adolescence through to adulthood.

Reminiscing is something U do quite often ... in fact, U sometimes do it too often.

Do U know **WHY**?

Because U feel safe and secure with what U know!

So U **DWELL** on things of the past and talk about... 'what U did when ...' or 'how U used to be ...', U even talk about ... 'if only U could put back the clock, U would ...', this process is perfectly healthy and valuable as long as we don't get lost in the **REMINISCING**.

That would be too easy, when U talk about how your past or past events have been responsible for shaping your life to date, or who U have become, U need to use the knowledge that U have extricated from the reflection process as the platform from which U will step off as U chart your path forward.

The message here is, quit dwelling on what was or wasn't and moping about what U should've, could've and would've changed if it hadn't been for ..., and get on with living your life today and into the future, achieving your ultimate goals and target[s] knowing and believing that because of where U have come from U are guaranteed to go the **DISTANCE**.
If U want to get something meaningful out of your reflection exercise then U need to do it properly and make it a life audit.

*NOTE
There are some simple exercises for U to work through as U read the rest of the reflection stage. These are significant visual aids.

Life Audit

This is not some complicated mathematical process that is going to leave U brain dead so don't get put off.

Put quite simply it's a process where U account for what U have done in your life from as early as U can remember, up to date, making note of key activities and time periods that have effectively been responsible for shaping what U have become ... good or bad.

Why would anyone want to do an exercise like this U may ask?

Your immediate reaction is ...'it only brings back into the forefront of your mind some things U probably feel U would prefer to forget.'

Yes, maybe U are right, but the **FACT** still remains that whatever has happened to U in your life from the beginning of time to date has a very **SIGNIFICANT IMPACT** on what U have done and become, and what U **STILL** have the **ABILITY** to **DO, ACHIEVE** and **BECOME**.

Are U ready for this?

If U are good to go, let's **DO IT**!
[see personalised sheets at the back of the book]

Step 1 Break your age down i.e. what U did between 2-5 years old, 6-10 years old, 11-15 years old etc as recollection of past activities is easier if it is done over shorter time frames.
This way U are more likely to remember key activities that took place, as they took place when U associate them with the specific age that U were at the time.

Step 2 **Highlight** any specific times and activities in your life that U feel have had an impact on where U are now and who U have become.

Step 3 With the information that U now have about yourself staring at U in the face can U indicate 3 possible directions that U could likely head in.

Step 4 Which is **the** direction for U, **highlight** it. Take a deep breath, then look again at the direction and use a different highlighter to pinpoint where U are at this present moment in relation to where U want to be.

Now use another highlighter to plot a dotted path leading U from where U are to where U want to be and along the path, write these words **BOLDLY, ...**

'**I KNOW I CAN GO THE DISTANCE**',

commit yourself to saying these words to yourself daily.

From this moment on, U will gradually begin to believe them, then U will start to actualise **them**.

WELL DONE, if U managed to work your way through this exercise. U will likely be feeling some mixed emotions.

This is perfectly normal, so please submit yourself to your emotions, and allow yourself to feel however U do.

Tell yourself that since moving forward is your object, then to reflect is good.

Now before U say **BYE BYE** to the Reflection stage, U have one last thing to do.

I always feel this part is quite fun and may even appear slightly silly to some, but when U remember how human nature works in relation to how much easier it is for U to believe the things U see, U will come to understand the validity of this exercise and why it is used to conclude the Reflection Stage.

Life Maps

Since I am operating on the assumption that we all have a general idea of what a map is, it makes explaining this exercise a lot easier.

That is not to say, however, that U are about to embark on one of those design classes where U will require compasses, protractors and all the works, so **FEAR NOT**!

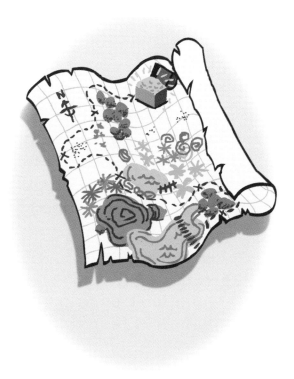

Instead, your tools of trade will simply be a single sheet of paper and some coloured markers, depending on your personal preference, for simple or busy creations.

*[see personalised sheets at the back of the book]

Next, with the information from the life audit, develop it into a **pictorial map** that can only be explained by **U,** the person who has created it making it very **PERSONAL** and **RELEVANT**

The underlying purpose of this exercise is for U:

- to have something tangible;

- that has meaning [i.e. when you look at it, U immediately understand it];

- that no-one else can understand [which safeguards your privacy and vulnerability];

- that U can use to commit yourself to in the future, and that U can reflect on and use in any **OTHER** way U can think of, towards getting U where U want to be.

This exercise is not about me or about impressing me it's about U.

Its not about getting it right; it's about U **STAYING FOCUSED** and **ON TRACK**, I would love to see the extent of creativity that U are all capable of developing, but unfortunately, it would not have a lot of meaning to me because it is a map about your life and not mine, so... at a glance ...

I couldn't decipher and analyse what the peaks, dips, dots, circles, lines etc mean without knowing and understanding U ... the map creator ... more intimately, something which time unfortunately does not permit.

THE IN-BETWEEN

'the place where your mind is deciding'

STAGE TWO   RELEASE
All The Reasons Why…
'didn't happen
[seeing through the tears]

[**Release** – free, let go, give up, surrender, discharge, relieve, liberate, emancipate, remit, pardon, rescue, acquit, retrieve, redeem, release etc I'm sure the list of all the other words U associate with **release** is extensive].

In this stage, U **have to recognise the need** to **release** yourself from the **reflection** stage in **order to move forward** and **resolve** what your plan of action is for your **LIFE**.

Part of this **process involves the apportioning of** blame somewhere [*normally not with yourself*] and looking at the reason why your life has turned out the way it has instead of how U think or feel or believe that it should have turned out.

Why do U do this?

Most of the time, because it makes U feel better and U feel that at least there is justification for your actions to date.

This way, U can convince others and possibly yourself that U are a rational and logical person even when U know the opposite to often be the case.

The pain of **REALITY** is all too much to bear when U admit that U haven't been thorough and thought things out properly before diving in and finding out U are in at the deep end.

It is less hurtful when U can lay the blame elsewhere.

<u>Ever heard of being in **DENIAL**?</u>

Oh! Yes **INDEED**.

That isn't to say, though, that for whatever reason things didn't happen, U don't feel the pain of:

- wasted time, opportunities, privileges;
- relationships, contacts;
- disadvantages;
- inabilities;
- lack of information or misinformation;
- a lack of patience and perseverance.

Just to name a few of the really familiar feelings.

The one question I normally ask at this stage is:

'If U could put back the clock, what would U change or do differently?'

The response is normally an extensive list of things, and most of the sentences sound like this:

'I would make sure that I ...';
'I would change the way I ...';
'This time around, I wouldn't let anyone ...';
or
'I would use every available opportunity to make sure that I ...'.

Take note here that the really interesting part of this response is the shift in **WHO** will be in charge and taking responsibility the second time around.

Even though U sometimes loathe admitting to yourself where U have failed, the details contained in your action plan for the future is a good determinant of whether any valuable lessons have been learnt from past experiences that will have a positive and significant impact on your future development.

How Much More ... Can I Take?

The truth is every one of us has been through the mills at some point in our lifetime, some more so than others and some more than U could possibly imagine, The aftermath of life's lessons can either be:

- a positive step in the right direction; Kudos to those who have had the strength to propel themselves in that direction;

or

- a negative state of mind accompanied by a pessimistic outlook where U reflect and get lost in the world of 'whys' and 'if only', the despair builds up and U become blinded by what U see as being a hopeless and helpless situation.

In the latter case, U know for a fact that things
cannot remain the way they are, U know
U owe it to U to pull yourself out of the rut,
get moving on and up.

Sometimes U even feel if U do **nothing**, it will all stop
and go away...**WRONG**, it won't.

Ever been told, **'U can run, but U can't hide'**?

Remember this when U ask yourself:

'How much more ... can I take?

The only way anything is going to stop or change is
because ... **U** make it stop, or **U** change it.

Ultimately, it all comes back to **U**, depends on **U**, and
will happen because **U** have decided it will happen.

So **U** make **THE** major decisions in your life ...

U want to do **SOMETHING** to change

EVERYTHING, but **what** and **how**?

With this flurry of thoughts going through your mind, U also have mixed emotions, which usually border on the negative i.e. anger, pain, anxiety, frustration and despair.

At the onset, these feelings are directed at **everyone** else that got in the way of things going RIGHT.

The more U get yourself worked up, the more hurtful it becomes and U switch from blaming everyone else to self-battery, where U start to blame **yourself** for making a mess of things in your life.

U tremble and feel like doing all sorts of things, most of which are best left off the pages of this book.

Suffice to say it doesn't look too good.

As the heat of the moment begins to simmer, U do something that we **SHOULD** all do from time to time,

U **CRY**.

Ti a ba nsunkun aa maa riran

I bet U are saying to yourself, 'that is too difficult to say' eh?

That depends on what languages U speak.

In this case, I have chosen to use a Yoruba adage which when translated means:

'while U are crying U will see clearly'

or more simply put it means:

'seeing clearly through your tears'.

This is one of my firm beliefs and something that I share with people who attend my self-development training programmes.

The two facts about crying, which U can't ignore, are:

- That crying is a natural body function;

- U all have the natural ability to do it.

At this stage, I'd like to ask U to do a little exercise and record your responses to the following questions.

[see personalised sheets at the back of the book]

*Please Note
It is very important to your own self-development needs that U are as honest as possible in your responses:

1. ask yourself why U cry

2. when last did U cry

3. when last did U have a **GOOD** cry

4. clearly state how U feel after U have cried

Look at what U have recorded as your responses.

Did U expect your responses to be any different?

Did U find crying therapeutic?

Hold on to this revelation about your responses for now.

For the purpose of this book, I have decided to re-affirm the significance of crying as an essential part of this release stage.

If U are the kind of person who is inclined to cry [*and, NO, I'm not going to insist that U cry, that is something that U are perfectly capable of without me instructing U*] stop for a moment and think about what happens when U cry, U will be surprised to see just how active your mind is throughout the whole cry.

Your mind is busy trying to sort out every thought, place things into a logical sequence and a plan of action all at the same time.

Exhausting, don't U think?

Isn't it funny when U think about all the people you've ever seen bawling out their eyes, and yet not once has it occurred to U that behind the scenes lie an extremely active mind.

<u>Wow!</u>

If at the end of your cry your mind hasn't sorted itself out and made any firm decisions about where and how U plan on moving forward, it isn't the end of the world … U are definitely on course, U just may not have realised it yet.

U will still, however, derive the benefits of the inner calm, which normally accompanies the relinquishing of all inhibitions to the eruption of your emotions as U submit yourself to your natural emotional state.

Some people think that crying is a sign of weakness, in fact this theory was for a very long time enshrined deeply in The 'Macho Man' Ideology and it was a major **NO NO** for all those that wanted to be followers.

As a matter of fact, in certain cultures, there was … and possibly still is … the belief that men do not and should not cry.

I however have never subscribed to that belief, at least not since I was eight years old.

Let me share a very personal experience with U, this is about a moment in time that touched me in a special way.

'A typical day in my life, my father would pick me
up from school and take me home for lunch.
We would eat lunch together, as was the custom,
after which he would freshen up
and go back to work.
This time was different, unbeknown to me
he had received a letter that was to change his life
and ... inadvertently ... ours forever.
While he was in his room freshening up, he must
have brought the letter out and re-read it
hoping that what he was reading wasn't true.
When I walked into his room to ask him something
[which I can't remember now], I saw him
sitting there on the edge of his bed
with head cradled in the palms of his hands,
... and he was **CRYING.**

*My little heart wrenched and I ran over to him, held his head in my tiny hands and told him not to worry, that whatever **IT** was*
*I would make **IT** better.*

*I didn't know then what **IT** was but that didn't seem to be my immediate concern, this was*

MY DADDY CRYING!

Daddies **DON'T CRY**, or **DO THEY**?

I'll never forget how I felt afterwards, I kept rolling the scene over and over in my mind, he seemed to be okay after a while, but he had still **CRIED**.

All these thoughts were going through my head at the same time:

- 'that means he hurts like me',

- 'it's okay for men to cry', and

- 'even if he does cry, it doesn't stop him from being my daddy'.

He eventually told me what had made him cry and how we would have to re-adjust our lives, he said all he could think about while he was crying was 'what to do next', and that 'his mind was working like clockwork'.

I'll never forget that he wasn't ashamed to **CRY**, this has always inspired me to encourage others when they need to cry to do just that.

THE END

'the place where **U** decide'

STAGE THREE RESOLVE
I Feel Good-self-belief: [the power behind going the distance]

Well that was certainly hard work.

If you've stuck with me this far, U know there is no going back!

Ever heard the saying 'Forward Ever Backwards Never', there is only one way from here:

FORWARD

At this stage, U start to feel some excitement because U know you're on to a winner *this* time ... its not about a bet, its not about a race, it's about **YOUR LIFE**.

What makes this time around any different from the numerous other times you've tried and failed to pull yourself back on to your feet?

What would U say if I said that the structured process of reflection and release is responsible for the buzz U feel about yourself because it has set free your ability for U to **BELIEVE** in **YOURSELF**.

Would U doubt me?

This is your HIGH for which U are perfectly entitled, U earned it and U deserve it.

What makes this moment so important is that **re-awakening** of the knowledge about where U are coming from, along with where U **want to be**.

Yet again, I say to U,

'U Know U Can Go The Distance'

Through your reflections come the realisation of your potential and your abilities, the fact that your focus has never completely blurred shows you've never given up on yourself, which is a sure sign of the belief U have in your potential to achieve.

Equipped with this renewed self-belief, and acknowledging everything that you've gone through with the excitement that being focused brings, your next step is to chart your path, the one you've always seemed to veer off, but should have stayed on.

Decision Time

This is where U make a **Personal Agreement** to do whatever it takes in order to be everything and do everything U have the **POTENTIAL** for.

U have the power to fulfil this ultimate goal not stopping short until U achieve whatever U have set out to achieve. Declare this as a **SUCCESS**:

S-selecting your goal;

U-unlocking your negative thinking;

C-charting your course;

C-committing yourself;

E-expect difficulties like some past experiences;

S-sacrificing yourself;

S-sticking to IT.

For one quick and brief moment, take your mind back to stage one of this book where U embarked on a soul searching journey into your past, and try to recall the emotions that were unveiled.

If U can recall how your journey through that stage made U feel, and the silent resolutions U made to yourself about never ever putting yourself through ... again, then find your strength to succeed in the self-belief that U will go the distance and be a **SUCCESS** unto yourself.

Your Master Plan

What is your Ultimate Goal?

Write it out somewhere; don't keep it secret so that if U don't achieve it, U can pretend it never existed.

Using your Life Audit, do a **Skills Audit**, to see what U have and what U don't have that U need to have in order to achieve your ultimate goal in life.

Can U determine how much of what U are lacking U need to acquire?

This way, U can plan your time wisely and specify when U will be ready to let All Systems Go.

Ask yourself if U are being completely honest with yourself in what U have set out to achieve, so that

U don't waste any more precious time chasing dreams.

What are the options for U to acquire the skills
U don't have?

Are there cost implications?

If so, what are the options for payments etc.

What time frames are involved, and will achieving
your goal require U to do a major u-turn in your life
style?

Answering all these questions honestly will
demonstrate whether your Ultimate Goal in life is
SMART:

S-specific,

M-measurable,

A-achievable,

R-realistic

T-timebound.

From now on, U need to ensure that **everything** U do is geared towards your success in life, particularly, your skills list of:

- 'to be done'

or

- 'to be achieved'

in order to go the distance.
Your final lesson has been the resolve to take personal responsibility and be accountable for your own life.

... distance here U come!

YOUR WORKSHEETS

YOUR LIFE AUDIT

STEP 1

STEP 2

STEP 3

STEP 4

YOUR LIFE MAP

RESPONSE 1

RESPONSE 2

RESPONSE 3

RESPONSE 4

... distance here U come!

MY FINAL WORDS ON THIS...

Ẹghẹ na ya rhiore, ẹ rọ rowiẹ

is a Benin [Nigeria] saying
which translates into English as...

'whenever U **WAKE UP,** that is your morning'.

So I say Good Morning to U!

You've just '**WOKEN UP**' and realised that a lot of precious time has passed U by because of all the issues around your self-belief.

You'd love to recapture all that lost time but the reality is that U can't.

All is not lost though because **now,** U have had the opportunity to re-visit what U once felt, and you're itching and rearing to go. Now it's all up to U.

At this point, U resolve that U are going to make **IT**, in order to make sure that U don't let any more precious time pass by, without being able to account for what you've done with it, U get ready to **START.**

Just as U set out to start, something stops U ... **How** do U go forward?

How hasn't mattered up to this point, because you've been too busy with excitement over the fact that U **Are** moving on.

Now U **need** to focus on getting the **HOW** right.

At this point U believe that there is 'A WAY'.

Now U want to know what it IS!

I know just the place where U will find useful tips on getting the HOW right,

and if U enjoyed reading this book
then U Will enjoy reading about the HOW
in ...

'U STEP TO WALK... THEN RUN'

by AH-TT.

COMING SOON!

AH-TT has prepared the next book in this series.

If you want to know more, please contact the publishers for further details:

**Distinctly Different Books and Publications
29 Dairy Close, Willesden
London NW10 3RJ**

www.ah-tt.com
e-mail: info@ah-tt.com

U STEP TO WALK...

THEN RUN

BY

AH-TT

ILLUSTRATIONS BY TOLU SHOFULE

SOWING THE SEED

AH-TT has decided to deliver this message
in the format of a book, being convinced that
the clarity and simplicity of its presentation
will touch the reader, and trigger them
into finding enough of that inner strength
and resolve to make a difference,
and go whatever distance they need
to go in their lives